VINTAGE
POSTCARDS
FROM THE
AFRICAN
WORLD

ATLANTIC
MIGRATIONS
— AND THE —
AFRICAN
DIASPORA

Jessica B. Harris, Series Editor

VINTAGE POSTCARDS FROM THE AFRICAN WORLD

*In the Dignity of Their Work
and the Joy of Their Play*

Jessica B. Harris

UNIVERSITY PRESS OF MISSISSIPPI / JACKSON

Furthermore:
a program of the J. M. Kaplan Fund

The University Press of Mississippi is the scholarly publishing agency of
the Mississippi Institutions of Higher Learning: Alcorn State University,
Delta State University, Jackson State University, Mississippi State University,
Mississippi University for Women, Mississippi Valley State University,
University of Mississippi, and University of Southern Mississippi.

www.upress.state.ms.us

Designed by Peter D. Halverson

The University Press of Mississippi is a member of
the Association of University Presses.

Publication of this work was made possible in part by a generous donation from
Furthermore, a program of the J. M. Kaplan Fund.

Manufactured in China
First printing 2020
∞

Library of Congress Cataloging-in-Publication Data available

LCCN 2019952253

Hardback ISBN	978-1-60473-566-6
Epub single ISBN	978-1-4968-2769-2
Epub institutional ISBN	978-1-4968-2768-5
PDF single ISBN	978-1-4968-2770-8
PDF institutional ISBN	978-1-4968-2771-5

British Library Cataloging-in-Publication Data available

For Those Who Came Before

&

For Those Yet to Come

&

For My Parents, Always

&

For My Families through Blood, Affinity, and Affection

&

For HSDC, who knows why

&

For the Next Generation:

Serenity, Garvey, Felix, Amalia, Olushola, Olukayode, Rafael,

Leonard, Henry, Peter, Temiola, Fiola, Xiomara, and Joshua

With regard for the past, love in the present, and hope for the future.

81. - Dans la Brousse.

Tamatave.

CONTENTS

ACKNOWLEDGMENTS

The list of acknowledgments could be as long as the text. So in order to keep that from happening, let me thank the entire staff of the University Press of Mississippi, current director, Craig Gill, and former director, Leila Salisbury, who believed in me and in this project.

Then I must thank family, friends, and colleagues who have aided, assisted, and abetted me in the formation and maintenance of my postcard collection. You know who you are and so do I. **Thank you All!**

VINTAGE
POSTCARDS
FROM THE
AFRICAN
WORLD

BECOMING A COLLECTOR

Adeltiologist is someone who collects postcards. I have spent more than fifty years of my life as a postcard addict roaming the world, always on the lookout for the little piece of pasteboard that would complete my collection, add another valent to its scope, or just plain make me smile with delight.

My first postcard collection was made on my first trip to Europe in the summer of 1963. Then, I traveled with my parents. Faithful tourists, we'd divided out souvenir tasks into three disciplines: still photographs, slides, and movies. It was an extremely well-documented trip, but it was truly notable because, like many tourists had in the past, I discovered postcards.

I became obsessed with the pasteboard rectangles, amassing a collection of the wish-you-were-here views as we traveled. There was the Eiffel Tower in Paris, the Baptistery in Florence, and Michelangelo's *David*—multiple views! I also began to collect images of the works that I loved in the museums we visited, of my favorite street corners, and more.

That collection is long gone, thrown out in one of the many purges that have marked my life. The images were the usual ones notable for nothing more than the fact that they were the catalyst that brought me to postcard collecting in earnest several decades later.

That journey would begin as I was working on my doctoral dissertation. The subject was the French-speaking theater of Senegal, and I journeyed to the West African nation to do my preliminary research. In the early 1970s, a Frenchman named Michel Renaudeau lived on Gorée Island off the Dakar coast. I never met him but heard that he'd created several books of antiquarian postcards of West African scenes from his own postcard collection. I found a copy of one of the books in a Dakar bookstore, and with one glance I was hooked on the older postcards, realizing that they presented a vivid photograph memorial that documented the way things were as nothing else could. Many were images taken by François-Edmond Fortier, a Frenchman whose name I did not know at the time. In his images, the dusty streets of Dakar's past sprang vividly to life. The tentative smiles of the newly circumcised young boys in their homespun garments with their Phrygian caps on their heads looked out across the years. The tam-tams that he recorded seemed like those that still-closed neighborhood streets in the Medina down in honor of baptisms. The architectural changes were fascinating, as were the images of early twentieth-century colonists strolling in their bustled skirts and solar topees. I was captivated by the postcards' abilities to bring the world of Africa's past vividly to life.

My friend Carrie Sembène (the then wife of the late Senegalese filmmaker) was an expert in all great things Dakar. She introduced me to an antique shop on a side street in the center of town that went against the prevailing commercial tides of the early 1970s that decreed that visitors to West Africa were only interested in tribal art. This shop was geared more toward expatriate French taste than to that of the yet-to-arrive African Americans. (Later in the decade, *Roots* made a trip to the motherland a vacation ritual for many.) The small shop sold everything from intricately carved wooden bowls and old musical instruments to vintage hand-cut eyelet *Goréenne* shifts in pristine starched cotton. There, amid the dresses and the bowls and the rest, lurked a tattered box of postcards. I found one or two that I loved and purchased them, but it soon became obvious that my graduate student budget couldn't stretch to more than a few. I illustrated my dissertation with images from the postcard books and those few cards that I managed to find in my Dakar wanderings. But I became determined that I'd find a way to begin a true collection of antiquarian cards of my own.

As often happens, life intervened. I had my dissertation to finish and a career as a fledgling journalist to balance with my professional obligations as a college instructor. My love of postcards was put on hold for a few years until, as a journalist for *Travel Weekly* newspaper in the early 1980s, I was selected to go on a two-week bus trip through Belgium and France. The trip began in the Low Countries—Brussels to be exact. We did the usual things: a tour through the Grande Place, a chocolate factory visit, a walk by the Mannekin-Pis, and more. We also visited the Flea Market at Sablons. There, I saw my first European postcard vendor.

The person's stand was unlike the others; rather than the rich display of porcelains or furniture, glassware or rugs, this stand was nothing more than folding tables topped with filing boxes. One glance inside the boxes revealed the treasures. Each of the well-marked boxes contained postcards, masses and masses of old postcards of the kind that I had seen in Dakar. It was my "ah-ha" moment. Of course! Postcards were designed to be sent HOME! Home for most of the colonists was Paris or London or Brussels. There were more likely to be more cards lurking in attics and scrapbooks in Europe than in Dakar or Point-à-Pitre. I had learned where to look and so another phase of my collecting had begun.

In retrospect, there seemed to be a decade-by-decade ramping up of my postcard mania. The next huge jump would occur in the mid-1990s. My writing career had taken off in quantity, if not in cash, and I was at work on my fifth cookbook, *The Welcome Table: African American Heritage Cooking.* I was charged with finding illustrations to complete the work. I knew I wanted line drawings; that was no problem. Patrick Eck, a friend, created a wonderful series: illustrating pigs and black-eyed peas, okra and watermelons. But, I also knew that I wanted a few archival images that would convey the depth of history and give a picture of the past. Again, as I had in my dissertation, I turned to the vivid evocations of the past that postcards provided. However, to my horror, I was reduced to renting images from the usual photo stock houses at fairly expensive fees. It was the moment I was subconsciously waiting for. I finally had an excuse to purchase the cards that had long intrigued me. The logic that unleashed the dam of acquisition was why "rent" images when, for the same amount of money or often even less, I could own the image—my own little pasteboard piece of history? I was off and running. With the dedication of one truly driven by demons, I began to haunt the flea markets I had visited years before and on my annual visits to Paris became an ardent frequenter of the Puces de Cligancourt, Paris's venerable flea market.

The Paris flea market is located to the city's northern edge right outside of what were at one time the walls of the fortified city built by King Louis Philippe. Take the Métro to Porte de Cligancourt on any given Saturday or Sunday and be swept up in a tidal wave of people who exit the Métro and then head north like lemmings. Don't even bother to stop to stare at the faux African art or the used clothing arrayed on the sidewalk; that's not the flea market. Head beneath the underpass and on to the rue des Rosiers and the surrounding warren of streets and alleyways.

In the late nineteenth century, the rag and bone men (and women) established themselves there at the Cligancourt gate. The city's scavengers were there as both the legal *chiffoniers*, or rag men, as well as the less than legal *pecheuers de lune*, or midnight fishermen, as the folks who would have been right at home in Fagin's London were called. They established a lively commerce reselling the city's detritus in an early form of recycling. Gradually, the hunter-gatherers of the city's trash became bric-a-brac vendors and legitimate secondhand dealers and established themselves outside of the city's northern gates. The location outside of the city gates was doubly beneficial, as the hinterlands fell outside of the city's tax-collecting zone.

The unofficial flea market began between 1880 and 1890, but the first real steps to making the market permanent and prosperous took place in 1885 when roads were cut and paved in an attempt to better organize the traders. By 1901, there were plans for an official flea market, which was already popular enough to be pictured on its own souvenir postcard. The market then, as now, was a weekend affair with specific areas gradually being established, each with its own specialty. The first was Vernaison, started around 1920 by Romaine Vernaison. Malik would follow and specialize in secondhand clothing and old World War I uniforms. In 1925, Biron, the most elegant of the markets, was established; it dealt in antique furniture and fixtures that can be surprisingly high-end. The Puces continued to grow and today covers seventeen acres and numbers fifteen different markets each with its own personality and specialty.

Named for the nineteenth-century French politician, the outdoor Marché Paul Bert is located at the far end of the rue des Rosiers and surrounds the indoor Marché Serpette. The items are not as upscale as in Biron, and there is a wide selection of vendors including vintage-clothing dealers selling used Hermès Birkins and hard-side Louis Vuitton luggage as well as stalls with Old Paris porcelain plates, copper kitchenware, antique jewelry, and the mid-century modern "antiques" that I remember from my childhood. I found my bliss at these two markets where I discovered a few boutiques that sold ephemera including postcards.

The market's current weekend schedule was fixed after World War II, with the morning hours of Friday devoted to the *déballage*, or unpacking, when the vendors set up their stands. This is a time for dealers and specialists only with each one waiting to see what treasures will be revealed. Saturday and Sunday there is frenzied activity with Parisians and tourists, alike, coming to search for the cup to match *gran'mère*'s set, the perfect *buffet à deux corps* to set off the newly renovated kitchen, or a much-coveted Baccarat decanter for the sideboard. While I have indeed reveled in the bustle and crush of the Saturday and Sunday markets, I have discovered that the sleepier Monday market suits me best. Then, some of the stalls are closed, and the traffic is significantly reduced. But the dealers are relaxed, and there is time for chatting and room for some companionable bargaining.

For several decades, I journeyed to Paris often and made it to the flea at least once each trip. I was usually accompanied Mammadou Sy, a Malian friend whose designer's eye and artist's sensibility made him a perfect partner in crime. There were not always a lot of postcards, but there was usually a box or two. And I would dutifully riffle through the cards looking for those that depicted life in the colonies, be they in the Caribbean or in Africa. I returned from most trips with an envelope or two filled with images from the past.

I had also taken to purchasing a copy of *Pariscope*, then the weekly guide to all Parisian happenings, upon my arrival. The classic guide listed everything from movie times at all of the cinemas to museum shows and even announced auctions going on around the city. It is difficult to imagine my glee at discovering on one trip that there was to be an auction of postcards during my Parisian stay. It was to be held at the venerable Paris auction house, Drouot. Mammadou, delighted at being my coconspirator in this endeavor, promptly dared me to go to the auction and bid on something and vowed that he would accompany me to give me the courage to do so.

The visit to Drouot was fascinating. At that point, I'd never been to Sotheby's or Christie's in New York; I'd only been to country auctions that were very informal. Drouot is a Parisian powerhouse and one of the world's great auction houses. It was inaugurated in 1852 and has sold works by Renoir. The halls of Drouot are daunting, to say the least. Known for its sales of very high-end fine art, antiquities, and antiques, Drouot is home to seventy independent auction firms who conduct auctions or *ventes* in sixteen different halls. In addition to the brief mention in *Pariscope* like the one that I'd seen, the auctions are all announced in the weekly *Gazette de l'Hôtel Drouot*, a glossy magazine that is sold on Parisian newsstands and that immediately became my must-purchase publication.

The building itself was enough to put the fear of God in me even though we'd dressed in our best auction-going garb: cutting edge attire for him and a business suit and pearls for me. (We had to look reasonably prosperous!) Mammadou and I headed through the front doors of the building. It was quite the experience. Each room had an auction or viewing going on, and it seemed as tumbled and overstuffed as the country auctions I'd attended. But the merchandise was Louis XVI *bergères, Empire lits bateaux* and 18-karat gold jewelry. I discovered that Drouot is not only Paris's most venerable auction house, but it at times also serves as the attic-cleaning venue for many a French family who is getting rid of *gran'mère*'s tatty but signed antique furniture and *gran'père*'s collections. On the day of the postcard auction that we attended, there was a furniture auction going on in an adjacent room, and the hallway overflowed like Ali Baba's cave with ornate gilt and mahogany furniture and Aubusson rugs.

The room for the postcard auction had folding tables around the perimeter set with boxes filled with the numbered lots. And there were loads of them. Aside from the chairs in the middle, it looked a bit like the stalls in the flea markets. I hadn't arrived in enough time to check out the lots, just in time to get registered as solvent to a certain amount and then get ready to bid. I was fascinated to note that the audience was not made up of the swells that show up in auction scenes in movies. There was not a bespoke suit to be seen in the crowd. (Our auction-going finery even made us look better-heeled than most.) Rather, it was a group of older, intense men who were haggling over items for collections that they'd been building for years. Some looked as though they might be dealers getting ready to resell their gains later to folks like me at a shop or market stand. I learned that the world of postcards is a small and tightly knit one with each individual having his or her own specialty. Some only collect antiquarian postcards of views of the provinces of France where they were born, others specialize in views of different former colonies, and still others only want cards dealing with boats or with the SNCF national railroad.

As the auction began and the bidding mounted, I could see that despite their looking like small-time operators, these gents knew what they were doing, and they also knew the street value of each and every lot. They were bemused by my appearance: an overdressed black American woman who was interested in postcards and her African sidekick. *That*, they had never seen before. The fact that I was interested in ones from colonial Africa and the Caribbean was even more astonishing. I could see that the auctioneer was intrigued by me and allowed me to tentatively get into the bidding on one lot. It was not the best lot by far, but it did have a few of the type of postcards that the French call *scenes et types* that show typical scenes of life in France and around the world. The *scenes et types* postcards it seemed were the most sought after and fetched the highest prices. The gentlemen, while they by no means stopped bidding, took pity and at least allowed me to get into the game, and I actually won the lot of about fifty cards. I no longer remember the amount that I paid for the cards, but I do know that I left Drouot feeling as though I had conquered the world. Bidding at Drouot taught me another valuable lesson. The world of postcards is serious business, and there are real collectors willing to pay almost any price to attain the one card of that one view that completes or enhances their collection. It was a lesson I would remember.

My postcard habit was getting expensive, and I figured out that I'd better learn a bit more about the habit I was acquiring. My life-long motto has been: if it collects dust, I collect it! As a collector of everything ranging from snow globes to coin silver spoons, pink lusterware, and Old Paris porcelain as well as postcards, I've learned that my collector's methodology is simple. When I see one thing that I love and purchase it or receive it as a gift, I am fascinated. When I see a second one, I'll compare it to the first, and if it meets up with expectations I will purchase it. When I've got a third, it becomes a collection (and all too frequently a mania!). At that point, I need to know more about the object of my collecting passion, so I begin to buy books, read articles, and generally attempt to acquire as much knowledge as possible. So it was with postcards. In addition to the Renaudeau books that I'd purchased decades earlier in West Africa, I began to find books on the history of postcards. Names of producers became familiar, and I subscribed to *Postcard Collector* magazine—an American magazine for postcards collectors who I discovered are legion. As I increased my knowledge of the subject, I acquired a knowledge of postcards: about divided backs and undivided backs, dates of various postal rulings, different photographic processes, and the like. I even subscribed to the *Main Antique Trader*, which had occasional articles about postcards. I also learned about postcard shows in the US, attended some and subsequently realized that the subjects that I was most interested in were usually not in the boxes displayed at the American shows. Eventually, I found that my occasional purchases of French or British magazines were more helpful to what was becoming my particular postcard specialty.

Over the years, spurred perhaps by the need to illustrate some of my cookbooks (along with *The Welcome Table: African-American Heritage Cooking*; *The Africa Table: Tastes of a Continent*; *Beyond Gumbo: Creole Fusion Food from the Atlantic Rim*; and *Rum Drinks: 50 Caribbean Cocktails, From Cuba Libre to Rum Daisy* are illustrated with cards from my collection) my topic had narrowed down to postcards depicting Africans and Africans in the diaspora and food and drink: fishing, farming, vending, serving, and consuming. I also collected cards of festivities: dances, dinners, baptisms, religious and cultural ceremonies, and such. I had widened my scope from the former French and British colonies to include the largest former British colony of the all: the United States, but the American cards I could find at home were only rarely as old as the French ones that remained a particular fascination. For that reason, Paris remained my Holy Grail of postcard collecting.

The Louvre des Antiquaires was located off the rue de Rivoli facing the famous Grand Hôtel du Louvre and across the street from the museum. The antique mall was nothing like the dust-filled antique barns of the American South, Northeast, or Midwest. Rather, these shops were highly specialized boutiques with pricey rents to pay for their location and the privilege of operating alongside other high-end dealers in the heart of Paris's tourist district. Among those selling period furniture, first standard silverware, and antique jewelry that made me weep with its beauty, one dealer sold ephemera. On my initial trip, I bought two old French ration cards from World War II from him. (One is framed in my kitchen, and the second was a gift for Jacque Pepin, who said they reminded him of his youth.) On my second trip to the boutique, I noticed the file cabinets and realized that their contents were postcards, loads and loads of postcards. It became one of the first stops in my Parisian postcard searching. The cards sold by the vendor were often too high-end for my collecting and boasted prices in the thousands of francs and later in the equivalent Euros, but I could venture in to peek and, once in a while, indulge. I realized that there were antique dealers who sold only postcards, and that was indeed a revelation. Where did they get their cards? What kind of cards did they sell? What were the prices? I knew about the flea market postcard trade, and I knew about the auctions at the Hôtel Drouot. I also began to investigate ephemera dealers and other sources.

In the back of a French collectors' magazine, I found another postcard and ephemera specialist. The address was on one of the *quais* that line the Seine—a Right Bank address near the *quai* where the bird sellers hawked their avian wares, or so we thought. My trusted sidekick, Mammadou, and I headed out. Well, the address was not at all where we thought it was, and after a long hike along the Seine, we finally located a small dark shop under an apartment building in a street that was so quiet as to be forbidding. But we crossed the threshold and voilà—the mother lode. The elderly gentleman who clearly was a dealers' dealer seemed to have no public customers and was astonished to see us enter his shop. But, he was a businessman, and I've found that those who work in the world of postcards and of antiques in general seem to be a curious group who gladly accept anyone who has a bit of knowledge, a willing ear to listen to their tales, and shares their collecting passions.

Soon, the gentleman was pulling out albums of cards that looked as though they had not been disturbed in decades. His cards were well-filed, and he had an extraordinary number of them. He also broadened my collection by introducing me to some of the early-twentieth-century trade cards that also showed images of far off places and Africans in the diaspora involved with food: growing it, cooking it, serving it, and eating it. Several postcards from the early twentieth century he turned over to explain: "You see this sort of faded bluish-gray paper? This is *papier de guerre*." I learned from him that the thinner paper had been used during the paper shortages of World War I and was another way to date the cards of that period. We must have stayed more than a few hours, for when I left I had a rather thick envelope filled with postcards and trade cards, a wallet that was considerably lighter, and the sky had darkened with evening.

I have never regretted the tens of thousands of francs that I left with him that afternoon, for on my return trip to Paris a year later, the shop had disappeared as though a mirage. The cards that I purchased from him of farmers in the French West African colonies and of Guadeloupean women decked with headscarves and masses of gold jewelry are some of the most prized in my collection. I've often wondered what happened to him. Did he fall victim to Parisian gentrification and find that his rent no longer allowed his quayside location? Did the elderly gentleman die leaving his collection to be sold at auction? Had he simply moved to a new address that I didn't know and couldn't find? I have no idea of the answer, but almost a decade later, each time I ride by the Right Bank *quais* past the former bird sellers market, I often think of him and wonder.

My next foray into the Parisian world of postcard dealers took me into some of the most unusual spaces in Paris—the Passages. Built in the period from the late eighteenth century until the mid-nineteenth century, the Passages are a Parisian hidden joy. Originally conceived to offer Parisians a way through the city without having to deal with the vagaries of the weather, they provide special promenades into the past. The Passages are a series of covered passageways leading from Montmartre down to the rue de Rivoli that enable those in the know to virtually cross much of the Right Bank without stepping out into the major thoroughfares or getting rained on. At their inception, each passage offered a different type of commerce: they were the shopping malls of the early nineteenth century. Today, they provide a time-travel excursion into a Paris long gone, bathed in the special light that the overhead glassed roofs provide.

In the 1850s, Paris had over 150 passages, today only a handful remain. Some of them, like the Galérie Véro Dodat and the Galérie Vivienne have been gentrified and are super chic, offering restaurants and tea shops, designer boutiques, and small shops selling luxury items. Other passages are seedier and considerably run-down with printing shops and dry cleaners. Somewhere in the middle range of passages is the Passages des Panoramas.

In 1799, an enterprising American entrepreneur named William Thayer had two towers built in which he installed panoramas that displayed views of world cities and were the movies of those days. He created a passageway that enabled clients to reach them under the enclosed roofs of a passage. Today the panoramas are long gone (they were destroyed in 1831), but the Passage des Panoramas remains. It is Paris's oldest and now, more than two hundred years since its inception, houses an increasingly gentrifying range of shops and a growing number of boutique restaurants as the joys of the Passages are becoming more obvious to Paris's contemporary shopping public.

At the same time charming and daunting crossing the threshold of the Passages des Panoramas almost seemed to transport me to another world: Garance and Baptiste of *Les Enfants du Paradise* seem to lurk just around the corner. Indeed, the Passage des Panoramas was written about in Émile Zola's 1880 novel about Paris's demimonde: *Nana*. The Passage is one that connects with two others so that there is a wide range of walks. Originally, there was a synergistic commerce of used book dealers, print sellers, philatelists, and framers. Today, along with the increasing trendy restaurants and boutiques, the passage is still home to many shops selling used books, prints, old newspapers, and leather-bound volumes that hark back to the period when the Passage was built. Maréchal, the internationally known postcard dealer is located in the Passage. I stepped through the door of the small boutique and immediately sensed that they would have every postcard that I'd ever searched for and more I'd not known about. They did.

It was at Maréchal that I found the card of the Guadeloupean market women selling ice cream to two awaiting young men. It cost more than I had theretofore paid for any single postcard, but it was glorious, in pristine condition with a stamp and a date, and was a part of the series that I was hoping to complete. I thought of the gentlemen that I'd seen years earlier haggling at the auction at Drouot, calculated just how much money I spent, and bought the card. I have not regretted it for one single second. Maréchal in the Passages des Panoramas is still my go-to spot for any individual card that I *must* have, for which I am willing to pay serious money.

On the other end of the collecting spectrum, a decade or more back, I also discovered the Puces de Vanves. Located at the opposite end of Paris from the larger and better-known Puces at Clignancourt, Vanves is the combination of the best of a flea market and a secondhand sale of the kind that the British call a car boot sale. Unlike the more formal Puces to the north, Vanves is an old-school flea market: there are no permanent structures, rather a coming together of dealers on Saturday and Sunday mornings. They back their vans up to their assigned parking spots, unpack them at dawn, and set out their wares on tables or on tarpaulins on the ground. At midday, they are finished and repack whatever they haven't sold back into the vans and disappear, leaving an ordinary urban streetscape for another week. But for the six hours or so of market each weekend morning, the vendors who occupy two bisecting streets on the southern outskirts of the city display everything from textiles and rugs to furniture. Limoges porcelain, Baccarat glassware, and a wide array of vintage kitchenware can also be found. There are used books and the graphic novels that the French call BD. Most importantly, though, there are usually several vendors who have a stock of postcards and at least one postcard dealer whose boxes can reveal treasures. It's old-fashioned collecting, rummaging, and rooting about, and I am never in Paris on a Saturday or Sunday morning without heading there at least once.

My collection has grown so that it now is housed in six leather shoeboxes. French cards from Africa and the Caribbean still dominate the collection, but all of my cards are not French. I have other Caribbean scenes from Jamaica and Barbados, Puerto Rico, and Cuba, cards from Mexico, Brazil, and a few other spots as well. Then, there is an entire group of cards from the southern United States. Each area required a different collecting methodology.

Every European capital city has its used book neighborhood, and usually there are postcards lurking in with the secondhand booksellers and stamp dealers. Philatelist shops may also often have postcard dealers' shops nearby or often may even deal in both cards and stamps. I learned that the postcard dealers in London were near the book dealers on Charing Cross Road. I have found spectacular finds in a used bookstore on Martha's Vineyard, where I grabbed a vast collection of cards from Jamaica one summer for twenty-five cents each. Boot sales in England and yard sales in the US have yielded a good assortment of cards as well. The British usually have cards from their former colonies and the French and Belgians from theirs. Cards that don't fit the national postcard profile are often cheaper, so I buy French cards in England, if possible, and vice versa. I've been collecting long enough to know that I do not often find cards like those that I discovered in my early years. But the rare finds do still occur, and as with most rabid collectors I live for the hunt. Although I have not yet gotten into trading cards, many collectors do, and I have also had a few cards in duplicate from points when purchase was irresistible because of a low price of a pristine card awaiting the moment when I begin to trade.

Like almost everyone these days, I have purchased cards on eBay. But I have found that I love the thrill of the chase, and I also need to examine the card. I want to hold it, see if it has flaws or creases or a nicked edge. Also photos do not always convey the texture of the paper, which is often a key to the card's age. I have also purchased cards online from bidStart.com, where there are several dealers who have amazing stock, but again, unless the card seems extraordinary, I miss the excitement of discovery and the delight in rummaging through a box and discovering something that I've been looking for.

In the United States, antique barns where several dealers trade under one roof are usually good spots for finds, especially in the Midwest. There, I found that while black memorabilia has become highly collectible and many search for images of blacks, there seem to be few looking at the culinary side of things. On a speaking engagement in the Midwest, I was taken to one of the region's numerous antique barns and delighted in discovering several dealers with boxes of postcards. There, the subject matter, though, was more about the American South, but they had a wealth of images, although of a more recent date than those that I collect from Africa and the Caribbean in Europe. Some American dealers and vendors do have older cards. In New Orleans, I've found a few cards from the early twentieth century in a case at a dealer's stand in an antique warehouse, and there are boxes of postcards in many of the city's used bookshops. The subjects vary, but they're always worth a glance.

I discovered that looking for cards of African Americans in the United States' are fraught with problems as the images were designed to uphold the prevailing political attitudes. In truth, some are not only racist, but deeply disturbing. I have no cards of public lynchings. (Horrifyingly, they exist, turn up in some dealers' stocks, and were sold as souvenirs of the unspeakable events.) There are none of the astoundingly racist cards of young black children as alligator bait and caricature "darkies" in my collection. While I realize that there may be a need for them to be collected to demonstrate the mentality of others in times that I certainly hope have passed, I have stuck to this collecting creed. Some of the watermelon cards I own may skirt the edge and several of my chicken and possum cards are certainly borderline, but none of my cards ever cross over into the truly horrifying. They also demonstrate the on-going connection, however problematic, that those foods had with African Americans in the minds of the general public of their time period.

As many of my books since 1995's *The Welcome Table: African-American Heritage* that ramped up my collecting instinct have been illustrated with postcards from my collection, each new book offers the opportunity to broaden the collection's scope. This has allowed me to begin to do some visual cross references regarding work and agricultural, and culinary and vestimentary habits between Africans and their descendants in diaspora in the American hemisphere.

Finally, with way too many shoeboxes crammed full of cards in their archival sheathes and a file of ephemera, a fair knowledge of postcard history and their background, and a collection of research and reference books to guide me, I can say that I collect in six different categories. I have a collection of postcards about the city of New Orleans that shows that city's growth and development, another on the island of Martha's Vineyard, and a small number of cards of old New York City. These collections represent my curiosity about the history and development of the places where I live and have personal history. Cards of early-twentieth-century Paris and others of the same period of France and England speak to my love of history and my career as a former French teacher. One I simply call "Beautiful Women," speaks to my love of costume, textile, and the study of feminine adornment, while another contains images of the cotton belt of the American South, a subject of equal fascination.

The bulk of the collection remains images of Africans and their descendants in diaspora and their connections to food. These are the ones that are shown in this volume. Years ago, I broadened it to depict not only labor, but also festivities, dances both real and posed, religious ceremonies, and more—in short, the full scope of a wide section of the history of Africans and the African diaspora in the dignity of their work and the joy of their play.

Some of my cards were donated to the permanent collection of the Smithsonian Museum of African American History and Culture, where they are used for study and also in the exhibits. At one point I even created a line of blank note cards from images of cards from my collection, but I no longer produce it. I wish I could say that I am no longer collecting cards. However, I still journey to Vanves and to my favorite shops each time I am in Paris, and I am always on the lookout for cards in used bookstores and at ephemera dealers. I occasionally dip into some internet sites that I trust, and my two most recent cards are from them. If there were a postcard-buyers-anonymous group, I'd have to stand up and admit that I'm a postcard collector and I'm always on the lookout for a yard sale, boot sale, or *vide grenier* whenever I travel. I find it impossible to pass up a gorgeous card. I guess that's why I am a deltiologist.

SOUTHERN DINNER TOTER MACON, GA.

INTERROGATING THE IMAGES

·••●•·

A Dialogue with the Cards

Although I certainly claim to be a deltiologist, I am not a postcard scholar. I collected initially from curiosity and from a fascination with the way that the cards themselves seemed to capture something that had previously seemed unknowable to me: a look, a style, a manner, a moment frozen in time. My two most recent postcard purchases, however, highlight a question that I, and indeed most who look at the cards, have. What is the thing that the card is trying to explain or express? The first card was the usual type that I'd acquired over the years: a studio portrait of an adorable serious-faced young boy with a basket over his arm and what appears to be a dinner pail in another. His clothing is tattered and held together with a safety pin, and he has on a cap and the basket reads, "Mr. F. Patton." The notation at the bottom of the card reads "Southern Dinner Toter, Macon GA."

The second card is more explicit: it is the image of a young woman standing in an archway atop what seems to be rubble. An archway over her head reads, "M. Barnett, Office 40, St. Louis." The card is as inscrutable as the other until one reads the printed commentary in the white space in the area atop which the young woman is standing. It simply read, "The Old Slave Block in the old St. Louis Hotel, New Orleans, La. The colored woman standing on the block was sold for $1,500.00 on this same block when a little girl." The context is breathtakingly clear. There is much more to know but the contextualization of the card amazing! That is what was missing from most of the other cards in

BASHFUL BILLY AND SISTER.

6743. COPYRIGHT, 1902, BY DETROIT PHOTOGRAPHIC CO.

my collection. Lacking the small print, it was impossible to do more than guess at the meaning of the cards: to enter into a dialogue with the cards.

As I collected, what I felt the card "said" as much as what the card depicted was what drew me to postcards and directed my selection. In many cases, the card's unspoken yet very real dialogue with me as the viewer was what directed the selection of one card over another. Some cards intrigued because of their inscrutability. Certainly, when I saw the card "Bashful Billy and Sister," as with "The Southern Dinner Toter," I was taken by the charm of the card itself but then came the questions: Were the children street vendors? Were they models who posed for the photographer? What was in the baskets that they carried? Who were their parents? Who did they grow up to be? Where did they live? Why were they photographed at the turn of the twentieth century? What was the photographer attempting to portray? Each card brought its own set of queries.

The Old Slave Block in the old St. Louis Hotel, New Orleans, La. The colored woman standing on the block was sold for $1,500.00 on this same block when a little girl.

The answers to some of the questions could be guessed at and/or researched, but most of the cards themselves still held mystery and therein lay another level of their appeal. The nature of old photography (which was hardly state of the art at the turn of the twentieth century) led to another layer of questions. Were the cards taken in situ, or were they posed in studio? Were the models victimized or complicit in some way? Many of the answers we will never know except from conjecture.

Other cards fascinated because they clearly illustrated specific points of culinary or cultural history. The cards surrounding peanut cultivation in Senegal are good examples. Peanut cultivation might seem to be a benign illustration of local industry. In fact, it was a massive enterprise, and Senegal was at the center of a vast peanut oil trade mandated by the French colonial powers complete with taxes and tariff. The Senegalese people upon whom it was inflicted hated the trade. The seemingly innocuous card provides a textbook example of colonial exploitation. A card detailing the fish caught by Senegalese fishermen, with the caption that the fish would "make European fishermen dream," reminds of the size and variety of fish caught in the waters off Dakar in the early twentieth century that are no longer available today. A series of cards taken by French ethnographer, François-Edmond Fortier, about whom I

483. Afrique Occidentale — DAKAR
Un marché indigéne

Collection Générale de l'A.O.F., Fortier, Dakar - Reprod. interd.

would learn much, provides a panorama of a section of a West African market. Although most in the series are correctly captioned "A market in Dahomey," one of them is labeled "Native Market, Dakar." It is clearly mislabeled to any student of African dress and mores. (The bare-breasted women with short-cropped hair would never have appeared in largely Muslim Senegal.)

In other parts of the non-Western world, postcards captured images of the various colonial outposts of the European motherlands. The colonial postcards were designed for Western aesthetics and equally reveal all of the prevailing prejudices and predilections of their period: the voluptuous mulatto, the happy sugar cane cutters, and so forth. Many of these early postcards were of necessity posed whether by design or complicity. (Photography hadn't attained the freedom and flexibility that it currently has.) The American ones may be blatantly racist, but the European ones suffer from an equally skewed optic as Christraud Geary notes in "Different Visions. Postcards from Africa by European and African photographers and Sponsors" in *Delivering Views: Distant Cultures in Early Postcards*:

> In the second half of the nineteenth century physical and cultural anthropology emerged as major academic disciplines that also bolstered expansionist and

MARTINIQUE et GUADELOUPE. - Marchande de Simples

GUADELOUPE. - Marchande de Corossol

8. - GUADELOUPE
Marchande de Tablettes de Cocos

GUADELOUPE. - Marchande d'Acras

GUADELOUPE. - Marchande de Lait

GUADELOUPE. - Marchande de Cocos à l'eau

Planting Sugar Cane.   *Love from Gram...*

colonizing efforts. Photography soon became one scientific means to document and survey all aspects of societies that had come under colonial dominion.

Postcards helped to perpetuate and encode images of Africa, and they greatly appealed to the Western imagination. (147)

This colonial category includes a subcategory of missionary cards that were used for fundraising and designed to extoll the virtues and the charitable work of whatever particular religious order had commissioned them. These cards show nuns distributing food to children, mass weddings, and work being done on projects supported by the religious organizations. Colonial cards also show aspects of the life in the colonies and often use ethnographic images taken by individuals like François-Edmond Fortier (1862–1928).

Fortier was a French documentary photographer, editor, and ethnographer who published over three thousand postcards of French West Africa (*Afrique Occidentale Française*) during his lifetime. His photographic archive detailed his West African travels. He moved to Dakar in 1900. In 1902 to 1903, he explored Fouta-Djallon, then Haute-Guinée. In 1905 to 1906, he travelled in *Soudan Français* (today's Mali), visiting Kankan, Bamako, Djenné, and Timbuktu. In later years he traveled further south to today's Togo, Benin, and

Nigeria. There, in what was Dahomey, he recorded markets and also captured some of the only images of the last of that country's Amazon warriors—the women fighting squad of the Fon rulers. Fortier was not only a photographer, but also a publisher of postcards whose cards were sought after by collectors of the period and are highly valued today.

As Fortier was in West Africa, so was Poché in the French Caribbean. They and other photographers, both known and anonymous, created a visual catalog of images that captured the region as it was. Some published their own cards; others worked for notable postcard publishers of the period.

In the French Caribbean, a variety of photographers operated, none of whom were as prolific as West Africa's Fortier. Edgar Littée aka Phos (1866–1931) worked in Guadeloupe and Martinique and produced a stunningly beautiful series of studio portraits of street vendors. Adolphe Duperly, a Frenchman,

No. 89. Bannana Carrier,
Port Antonio.

"Greetings from Jamaica."   Loading Banana, Port Antonio, Jamaica.

along with his sons were pioneer photographers active in Jamaica. Their studio, established on King Street in Kingston, Jamaica, in 1840, published a souvenir volume *Picturesque Jamaica* that contained early photographs of the island, many of which were also reproduced as postcards. British postcard publishers, Tuck, one of the best-known businesses in the golden age of the postcard (1907–1915), produced a variety of cards in the English-speaking Caribbean and even some of the American South. A decade after their purchase, I discovered that two of the cards that I had long thought were of Caribbean sugar cane cultivation Caribbean were in fact an image of southern Louisiana.

Initially, the Fortier cards of western Africa predominated in my collection, but gradually, I discovered sources for cards from the Caribbean. There, the vicissitudes of life under the colonial system were also amply documented. Pulping Cocoa in Jamaica showed itself to be arduous work. A heavily ladened banana carrier revealed the other, less picturesque side of Harry Belafonte's "Day-O," and coaling in St. Lucia—provisioning coal for the boilers of the sailing ships—made the viewer aware of the harshness of life. A clearly posed portrait card from Martinique depicted a coal carrier for the Compagnie Générale Transatlantique with the handwritten notation that it is the women who do the work in Martinique and that each full basket of coal "weighs 46

Strawberry Pickers and Crates, NORFOLK, Va. 3054.
get to work negros what do I pay you for, on a strike Emma .

kilos and they get one sou per two baskets. They carry on average two hundred a day which makes about 10,000 kilos carried on their heads." In that case, the card, mailed in 1901, then becomes not only image, but a telling sociological document.

Some of my more expensive cards were photographed in a studio like the series of street merchants by Edit. Phos in Guadeloupe. With their precise poses and their attention to detail, they provide visual information on dress, jewelry, head ties, foods sold, and more. Scholars of the history of photography remark the manner in which the cards maintain and support the prevailing cultural, social, and political attitudes of their times and argue that neither the eye nor the aesthetic are those of the subjects of the images.

Eleanor M. Hight and Gary D. Sampson, in "Photography, 'Race' and Post-Colonial Theory," their introduction to the volume *Colonialist Photography: Imag(in)ing Race and Place*, state that

the overwhelming evidence of the photographs seen within the contexts of specific episodes of colonial history indicates that the images produced a dynamic rhetoric of racial and ethnographic difference between white Europeans and Americans and non-European 'races' and 'places.' The photographers expressed

OLD TIME KITCHEN & DARKEY (OVER IN DIXIE LAND)

distinctions between colonial peoples and themselves ambivalently; as agents of colonial culture, they most often envisioned their subjects as objects of both racial inferiority and fascination. (1–2)

Hight and Sampson are speaking of photography from "its first documentary uses to World War II"; however, when dealing with postcards, many of the paradigms remain the same as one of the primary ways of distributing the photographs was as postcards.

Captions printed on the cards for the most part describe the event or individual portrayed without comment or remark: a corner of the market, a religious procession, and so forth. When they do stray into the realm of commentary, they reveal prevailing European attitudes and are rife with condescension: an "elegant banana seller" or "strong partisans of sugar cane."

While one may rail at the colonial aesthetic of the European cards, cards from the United States are much more problematic. Often they are printed with captions that indicate the racism of their epoch. "Old Time Kitchen & Darkey" and "Coontown en Fête" are very moderate illustrations of these attitudes. Indeed, in looking for postcards, I came across cards of lynchings and acts of violence that were beyond disturbing and indicative of a national

163. SÉNÉGAL — DAKAR - Procession

Afrique Occidentale - SOUDAN

1118. Tam-Tam de Habbés (ces tam-tam sont allégoriques et présentent de nombreuses phases)

Collection Générale Fortier, Dakar

Going to sell the Pig.

attitude. In the American cards, there is an almost palpable delight inf portray-
ing the blacks in demeaning roles and documenting "picturesque poverty." The
comments on the verso of the cards also indicate a racism on the part of the
senders that at times surpasses that of the image on the front of the cards sent.
For example on the front of an early image of strawberry pickers in Norfolk,
Virginia, mailed in 1906, the sender has written, "Get to work negro's [*sic*] what
do I pay you for, on a strike Emma."

Occasionally, though, the messages indicate an ethnographic curiosity and
not a superior colonial contempt like the notation on a card sent from Trinidad
in 1908, "Always pleased to hear from you. This shows Indian immigrants men
and women on a cocoa estate. Note my name has no O in it. That's your only
mistake." (The signature is illegible.) The later part of the message reminds that
the cards were the major form of correspondence before telephones. Often,
there might just be a simple greeting from a traveler, "Leaving today for the

Collection Leray   15. - CONGO FRANÇAIS. - Vive la France toujours ! - Brazzaville

rest of the island, don't expect much mail. Hope the heat in Phila. is not too much for you. The pig in the picture might resemble my appetite. Mildred" with the additional notation in a different handwriting, "I think there will be a famine in Jamaica because Mildred has eaten almost all the food. Everything is O.K. M.A.P."

Then there is the question of the photographer's intent and the complicity, or lack thereof, on the part of the subjects. Some of the most important cards were photographed in the early part of the twentieth century when photography was still a developing art form. It involved cumbersome equipment and long exposures. Many of the postcards were actually photographed in studio and some in various versions as with the scene in a Moorish café photographed with and without the young boy. I do not have a complete set of the lovely and highly collectible series of vendors photographed by Edit. Phos in Guadeloupe, but they also seem to be studio posed. The idea of studio images then raises all manner of questions of relationships between photographer and subjects. Were there financial agreements? Were the subjects chosen for their "picturesque" aspects? If so, were these enhanced with props of any sort? The questions continue and are in most cases without resolution. In other cases, subjects seem to be caught in the midst of their daily tasks. In still other cases,

1516. - **Afrique Occidentale - Dahomey**
Danses de féticheuses

Collection générale Fortier, Dakar

Mo prends oune charme
Pour mo charmé fille-là ;
Mo réfléchi a rien de force pas bon ;
Mo prends charme-là
Mo jeté-le dans la mer...
Si p'tite fille-là content mo,
Li hé marché derrière mo.

(Air Créole)

37. - APPROUAGUE. - La Danse du « Gragé »

the images clearly display a deliberate patriotic zeal. The card from the French Congo showing young children around the French flag that proclaims, "Vive La France toujours," requires no explanation.

While, as a collector, I remained mindful of questions of photographers' intent and Europe's and America's view of the Africans and their new world cousins as the "other," it was not my immediate concern or reason for collecting. Other collections have been assembled and essays have been written about the colonial eye and the racist and sexist attitudes that are on display in the postcards. Bare-breasted women appealed no doubt to the prurient sensibilities of some viewers as did the images in *National Geographic* in a not-much-later period. There is much to be written about and discussed on that note. However, in my collecting I chose to focus not on the colonial eye, but instead on the details revealed in the images captured: the shape of a head-tie, the fabric of a dress, the gesture of a hand, and the use of a tool. The cards contained pictures of all aspects of material culture. In them it is possible to see art, craft, and design. I found myself intrigued by the woven texture of a basket; shape of a pot or jar; and twist of a head-tie, or *tignon*; or delighting in recognizing the classic African double-hitch of a skirt and the angle of a hoe blade. The cards even show social norms and cultural references like the nursing goat in a card from Cuba that made every older Cuban I showed it to smile with recognition.

While I concentrated on collecting images that depict people and food or in their relaxed moments, the cards also show destroyed buildings and streets long forgotten. A card of flower sellers in Adderly Street in Capetown, South Africa, shows not only the vendors, but also a double-decker omnibus with an advertisement for Flag cigarettes on the front. The traffic seems to have a combination of horse-drawn vehicles and motor ones and a streetscape that reveals the front of shops decorated with the complicated ironwork that is sometimes called *brookielace* (panty lace) in Afrikaans. The scene depicted in the card known as the call to prayer is timeless and can still be seen repeated in cities and small hamlets throughout Muslim Africa. The card of the newly circumcised boys reminded me of scenes that I had witnessed in the side streets of Dakar, Senegal in the early1970s in a now-past era.

As I collected, I was struck by similarities of pose and saw developing parallels among the categories: the market women in Senegal and their counterparts in Guadeloupe, Charleston, and Barbados. People preparing rice in Madagascar and in Senegal and kitchens large and small throughout the diaspora. There were other curiosities: an apparent fascination with bananas on the part of photographers yielded a raft of Caribbean cards depicting banana cultivation and vending, while sugar cane led to cards from Puerto Rico, Cuba, and New Orleans, all depicting parallel scenes from planting to harvesting. Some of them are virtually interchangeable because the worlds of labor were so similar.

In the United States, there were cards of the growing cities as well as others extolling the virtues of small town life, the changing landscape, and the bounty of the land. Then, there were those from the American South depicting African Americans at work and at play. These had a different feel usually from those of Europe. They were more vicious and visceral. Frederick Douglass stated, "Negroes can never have impartial portraits at the hands of white artists." Indeed, cards of the American South of the early period can be particularly racist with stereotypical images of indomitable mammies, smiling cotton pickers, negro idlers [*sic*], and black babies providing bait for alligators in Florida. Most of them provide more than ample fodder for a well-deserved screed on the racism. However, they are representations of the prevailing national standards of the post-Reconstruction period and detail America's prevailing racism toward African Americans.

As I collected, the cards gradually started to organize themselves, and I began to discern categories. There seemed to be a number that dealt with agricultural work and with maritime pursuits. These, I categorized as the Farm, the Garden, and the Sea. Another set examined huckstering and street vending and displays a wide variety of market practices including foods bought and sold in the market places and the markets themselves. These I labeled the Marketplace, the Vendors, and the Cooks. Finally, there were those that documented festivals large and small whether they were Roman Catholic religious processions or traditional dances on both sides of the Atlantic. These went into a section I called Leisure, Entertainments, and Festivities.

In attempting to find answers to all of the myriad questions posed by the cards, I found that I was transported into a world of the past only to realize that there were in fact no solutions, only moments of interrogation and of contemplation. In most cases, the cards offer a springboard for inquiry. The results are dependent on the expertise of the viewer and on the viewer's field of research. For me, the cards are windows to the past. They are literal snapshots of a moment—real or contrived—open to seemingly endless interpretations that change with time and place and point of view. They are ciphers that encompass the past and the present.

However, there is one thing that is undeniable whatever the interpretations may be. What *is* there, what *is* visible in each and every postcard is a record of a period, one in which people black and white came together in black and white to provide a lasting record of their flawed times for the future. They show the faces of those who have gone before, captured for eternity in the dignity of their work, the calm of their repose, and the joy of their festive occasions.

POSTCARD HISTORY

•◦•●•◦•

Postcards, a major form of communication from the mid-nineteenth century to the present, have long been a part of the fabric of our daily lives. The importance of postcards in the late nineteenth and early twentieth centuries is inconceivable in our present world of cell phones and email and social media, yet the postcard phenomenon documented the world's journey into the modern era and played a cardinal role in developing images and conceptions of other cultures during the latter third of the nineteenth century and the first third of the twentieth.

Developing in the 1860s and wildly popular by the early twentieth century, postcards and their images bear silent witness to just how times have changed even more than the messages they carry. In the United States, they document the growth of cities after the Civil War. In Africa and the Caribbean, they parallel the apogee and decadence of colonialism. The small rectangular pasteboard souvenirs house memory; they are photographic witness to a world that was, and is, no more.

The development of postcards and their popularity also parallel the growth and development of international postal systems. Until the middle of the nineteenth century, written communication took the form of business correspondence and other handwritten missives as well as the occasional *billet doux*. These were sent by couriers, private messengers, and the early, rudimentary public and private postal systems that were used by the elite. (These existed as early as China's Han Dynasty.) In the Western world, what we now take for granted as public mail service began in the United Kingdom only in 1840 led by Sir Roland Hill, who developed a system of penny postage that led to the codifying of the system, the development of postage stamps, and the opening of the postal service market to a rapidly growing literate middle class.

In the United States, the Second Continental Congress established the Office of Postmaster General in 1775 with Benjamin Franklin named the initial postmaster general. Prior to that William Goddard had set up a private inter-colonial mail service that included thirty post offices between Williamsburg, Virginia, and Portsmouth, New Hampshire, relayed by post riders employed by the individual postmasters. As the country expanded, so did the postal network, gradually becoming an arm of the government. Initially, postal rates were based on distance, but by 1845 the department began charging based on a combination of distance and weight. In 1863, rates were fixed and service became universal throughout the country.

Earlier, in 1861, in Philadelphia, Pennsylvania, John P. Charlton applied for copyright for a private postal card. He was granted copyright but was denied the patent he had also applied for. Discouraged, he sold his copyright to H. L. Lipman, who produced and sold a card with room for an address on the front along with a stamp that allowed for universal delivery and a place on the verso for a message. There were no pictures on the cards, but they were well used. Lipman is considered the father of the modern postcard. Similar cards were developed in Belgium, Germany, and Austria, where in 1869 the first government-sanctioned card was printed. The correspondence cards (as they were called) were extremely popular and widely used, and within the first three months of availability the Austrian government sold almost three million *Correspondenz Karte*. Following on the heels of European post offices, the American government began printing its own version of them by 1873. However, these cards were blank with only room for a brief message on one side and the address on the other and were subject to the same postal rate as a one-sheet letter. In 1875, as a result of an agreement made at the First International Postal Congress, they were allowed to be sent internationally after July 1, 1875.

Europe was in advance of the United States in that post offices there developed a cheap rate for postcards, which paved the way for the souvenir postcard. However, before souvenir cards arrived, there were advertising cards. The first printed advertising cards appeared in England in 1872 and in Germany in 1874. They had an advertising image of some sort on the front and room for an address on the back. Exposition cards, showing the main building of the

Inter-State Industrial Exposition in Chicago that debuted in 1873, were also created but all of these cards were commercial and not designed as souvenirs.

Souvenir cards with an image on the front and room on the verso for an address were the logical next phase. One of the earliest originated in Austria and was mailed in Vienna in 1871. Parisian cards with an image of the Eiffel Tower appeared in 1889 and 1890, foretelling the tidal wave that was about to occur. In the United States, souvenir cards debuted in earnest with the 1893 Chicago Columbian Exposition, and multiview cards showing several images of that location and others were produced and sold to travelers. With the turn of the twentieth century, postcard sending and collecting became an international mania ushering in the first major era of the postcard: that of the undivided back, which dates from 1901 to 1907.

Undivided back cards, which had no space for writing other than around the image on the front, began the extraordinary growth of card mania. The *Post Card Dealer*, an American trade journal reported that in 1906 alone 1,161,000,000 cards were sent through the post in Germany. The figures for the same year in the United States and Britain were 770,500,000 and 734,400,000, respectively. There were multiple types of cards ranging from humorous ones to images of beautiful women and cabaret and stage stars to risqué ones (the proverbial French postcards) to those that depicted classic locales on the Grand Tour.

By the close of the early phase of the souvenir postcard period, different countries began to allow space for writing on the back half of the card along with the address. England began in 1902, France in 1904, Germany followed suit a year later, and the United States finally entered the game in 1907, ushering in what is known as the Golden Age of Postcards, 1907 to 1915.

Postcards of this period, with their room on the back where a message could be written without obscuring the image on the front of the card allowed designers to give flight to imagination, and cards of all types emerged—some embellished with ribbons and fabric, others with plant material, and still others with whatever would make them unique and salable. Many of the cards were produced in Germany, where the printing technology was considered to be the state of the art. Costing less than a letter to mail, cards provided a cheap and quick method to remain in touch with friends and family members across towns and around the world. A quick perusal of some of the messages newly allowed on the backs of the cards show that they were used for all sorts of news, ranging from travel news of impending visits and safe arrivals to brief descriptions of the mundane occurrences of daily life. Some even offer commentary on the scenes on the card's front. These souvenir postcards of the Golden Age had the international impact of telephone, email, Twitter, and Instagram combined for the world's citizens in the pre–World War I period.

The advent of World War I slowly brought the golden era to a close. The war produced shortages and even the paper declined in France, becoming a thinner grayish blue that in France is known as *papier de guerre* (war paper). Some of the earlier card images continued to be reproduced in the new divided back format, but by the war's end, the world had changed. The advent of the telephone and easier communications ensured that the postcard's glory days were over. Postcards never again attained the worldwide popularity of the Golden Age, but even today at tourist spots around the globe it is not hard to find a pasteboard card with an image on the front on which a traveler can scribble a hasty note home saying, "Wish you were here!"

DATING POSTCARDS

Postcard history is fluid and the dates of various periods depend on the individual country. Even then there is no consensus on dates as postcards of any particular type could be mass-produced and were sold until the stock was finished, which might result in cards being sold in multiple periods in decreasing volume. Also many popular images were reused over several periods. General dates adapted from the Smithsonian Institution's Archives online history of postcards run as follows:

PIONEER PERIOD, 1870–1898

This period includes advertising cards, exposition cards, and some of the other precursors to the more traditional postcard.

PRIVATE MAILING PERIOD, 1898–1901

This brief period includes undivided back cards. Some were marked as "Private Mailing Cards" to distinguish them from government-produced cards, which often had the phrase "Postal Card"—*Carte Postale* printed on the verso, which meant that it could be used in the international postal system.

POST CARD PERIOD, 1901–1907

This period is also known as the undivided back period because messages could not be written on the address side of the card. Again, the phrase "Postal Card"—*Carte Postale* printed on the verso meant that the postcard could be used in the international postal system. The era began to include photograph cards using real photographs attached to premade backs that could be sent through the mail.

DIVIDED BACK PERIOD, 1907–1915

In 1907, the Universal Postal Congress decreed that cards produced by governments of member nations could have messages written on the left side of the verso. Within the year, these rights were also extended to private producers of cards. Postcards could be used to convey simple messages, which gave a huge boost to the postcard industry. These divided back postcards and the messages that they conveyed around the world made postcard usage even more popular and ushered in what has come to be known as "The Golden Age of the Postcard." Transitional cards of the earliest phase of this period asked the sender to check to make sure that a message can be included on the back.

WHITE BORDER PERIOD, 1915–1930

With the beginning of World War I, Germany lost its primacy in the production of postcards and the United States took over, albeit without the same technology. Both the quality and the quantity of postcards declined. Ink was saved by not printing to the card's outer border giving the period the name of the White Border Period.

LINEN PERIOD, 1930–1945

The 1930s saw the introduction of printers that could produce postcards with high rag content and a linen-like feel. Brighter dyes for the increasing number of color cards and quicker production became hallmarks of these cards, many of which still retained the white border.

Subsequent periods include the photochrome period that dates to the present and a second wave of advertising cards that date from the late twentieth and early twenty-first centuries. None of the postcards in my collection date later than the White Border Period.

Postcards may also be dated from their size, which was also regulated by post offices:

> In the early stages of postcard production, government-produced postcards varied in size, depending on the type of postcard. Privately produced postcards, also known as private mailing cards, did not need to adhere to the government restrictions. On June 1, 1878, the General Postal Union, an international postal

organization, signed a new treaty, changing its name to the Universal Postal Union. This treaty set the maximum size for postcards produced by governments of member nations at 3.5 × 5.5 inches.

The Private Mailing Card Act of May 19, 1898, stipulated that private mailing cards measure 3.25 × 5.5 inches. After 1901, postcards typically measured 3.5 × 5.5 inches, although variations in size exist (Smithsonian, "Dating Postcards").

Cards may also be dated by looking at the prices of the stamps used to send them. These can then be used to calculate relative dates by researching the postal regulations and postage prices in the various countries. If the card has been mailed, the postmark will indicate the date before which the card was produced, but card stock was not always up to date and the card may have been produced years earlier than the date on which it was mailed.

The cards in my collection come from a wide range of countries and time periods, and many of them have never been mailed. As I have collected only for pleasure and for the purpose of illustrating my books, I have made no attempt to undertake a detailed dating other than by the general postcard period and/ or the postmark if it exists. The cards are presented here without commentary or detailed analysis and cataloged as to place of origin with simple notations of the information printed on each card. A few were selected and the message on them either on the front or on the verso (if legible) is also recorded. It is hoped that readers will draw their own interpretations without a rigidly defined context. I am mindful that the possible interpretations and uses of the cards would be limited by attempting to define possible uses. I have collected them. I leave it up to the viewer to interpret them through their own chosen lens.

POSTCARDS

Africa

THE FARM, THE GARDEN, AND THE SEA

135. Afrique Occidentale – Sénégal – Saint-Louis – Guet N'Dar – Départ des pêcheurs. Mise des pirogues à l'eau et passage de la barre [*West Africa – Senegal – St. Louis – Guet N'Dar – Departure of fishermen. Putting pirogues in the water and crossing the bar.*] Collection Générale Fortier, Dakar. Back: Carte Postale. Tous les pays n'acceptant pas la correspondence au recto, se renseigner à la poste [*All countries do not accept correspondence on the recto, inform yourself at the post office*]. (Divided Back.)

246. Sénégal – Gorée – Vente du poisson sur la plage [*Senegal – Gorée – Sale of fish on the beach*]. Fortier, Phot., Dakar. Back: Carte Postale. Ce côté est reserve exclusivement à l'adresse [*This side reserved exclusively for the address*]. (Undivided Back.)

Back: Niafunke – Ces poissons, des "capitaines" feront rêver des pecheurs européens [*Niafunke – These fish, "capitaines" will make European fisherman dream*]. Heliogravure Rotative, Paris.

524. Sénégal – Rufisque – La Plage
[*Senegal – Rufisque – The Beach*]. Editions
Fortier. Fortier Photo Dakar. (*Undivided
Back. Mailed 1905.*)

Dakar – Le Port. Chargement des
Arachides [*Dakar – The Port. Loading
Peanuts*]. (Divided Back. Mailed 1907.)

58. Sénégal – Manutention des Arachides [*Senegal – Loading Peanuts*]. Fortier, Phot Dakar. Back: Carte Postale [printed upside down]. (Undivided Back.)

17 Gathering Grapes, near Capetown. Back: Post Card. This space as well as the back may now be used for communication Inland Postage only. (Divided Back. Mailed 1907.)

No. 9. Une corvée d'eau, femmes dahoméennes [*Dahomean Women Carrying Water*]. Collection Geo. Wölber. (Divided Back. Mailed 1908.)

106 Tunisie. – Lavage des Olives pour recueillir l'Huile [*Tunisia – Washing olives to collect the oil*]. Collections ND Phot. Back: Carte Postale. Ce côté est exclusivement reserve à l'adresse [*This side is reserved exclusively for the address*]. (Undivided Back.)

Zambèze – Vannage du grain [*Zambezi – Winnowing grain*]. Back: Edit. Des Missions Evangeliques, 102, b. Arago, Paris. (Divided Back.)

Missions d'Afrique – Petits Garçons revenant du travail [*African Missions – Little boys returning from work*]. Back: Carte Postale. (Divided Back.)

Africa

THE MARKETPLACE

483. Afrique Occidentale – Dakar. Un marché indigène. Collection Générale de l'A.O.F., Fortier, Dakar – Reprod. interd.
[*West Africa – Dakar. A native market. General Collection, Fortier, Dakar – Reproduction Forbidden.*]. Back: Carte Postale.
(Divided Back.)

P. Grehert, phot., Casablanca. 7. Le Maroc pittoresque – Mauresque vendant du pain [*Moroccan woman selling bread*]. (Divided Back.)

1081 Boutique Arabe [*Arab Shop*]. (Divided Back.)

Flower Sellers, Adderley Street, Cape Town

Flower Sellers, Adderley Street, Cape Town. Back: Post Card. John G. Bain, 101 Longmarket Street, Cape Town. (Divided Back. Mailed 1909.)

6434 SCÈNES ET TYPES. — Femme arabe préparant le couscouss. — LL.

6434 Scènes Et Types. – Femme arabe préparant le couscouss. – LL. [*Arab woman preparing couscous – LL.*] (Divided Back.)

Africa

THE VENDORS AND THE COOKS

216. Algérie – Marchand de guimauve [*Algeria – Taffy Merchant*].
Back: Collection Idéal P. S. (Divided Back.)

37 Cuisson d'une Diffa. - ND Phot [*Cooking a Diffa – North African Feast*]. Back: Carte Postale. Ce côté est exclusivement reserve à l'adresse [*This side is reserved exclusively for the address*]. (Undivided Back. Mailed 17 August 1903.)

Dakar – Préparation du Couscous [*Dakar – Making Couscous*]. Back: Carte Postale. Tous les pays n'acceptant pas la correspondence au recto, se renseigner a la poste [*All countries do not accept correspondence on the recto, inform yourself at the post office*]. (Divided Back.)

Madagascar – Décorticage du riz [*Madagascar – Hulling rice*]. (Divided Back.)

203. Loanda Quitandeiras [*Vendors*]. Osorio & Seabras – Loanda – Editores. Back: Bilhete Postal Angola. (Undivided Back. Mailed 1906.)

Missions des P. P. du Saint-Esprit. Au Marché [*At the Market*] Back: Carte Postale. Phototypie J. Bienaime–Reims. (Divided Back.)

No.1. Une beauté dahoméenne [*A Dahomean beauty*]. Collection Geo. Wölber. Back: Carte Postale. (Divided Back. Mailed 19 August 1908.)

123. – Madagascar. – Diègo-Suarez. – Bourjanes vendeurs de Riz [*Bourjanes rice sellers*]. Editeurs Grand Bazar Charifou-Jeewa. Back: Carte Postale. Tous les pays n'acceptant pas la correspondance au recto, se renseigner à la poste [*All countries do not accept correspondence on the recto, inform yourself at the post office*]. (Divided Back. Mailed December 4, 1908.)

639. Scènes et Types. – Un Café Maure [*A Moorish café*]. Collection Idéale P. S. Back: Carte Postale. (Divided Back – *Papier de guerre.*)

Missions d'Afrique – Une Brasserie – La bière est composée de maïs et de blé. Cette boisson est capiteuse [*A Brewery – The beer is made of corn and wheat. This beverage is intoxicating*]. Back: Carte Postale. (Divided Back – *Papier de guerre*.)

Dans la Brousse. La Popote Indigène [*In the Bush – Native Food*]. Back: E. Dachel, éditeurs à Tamataye (Divided Back. Mailed 1914.)

Africa

LEISURE, ENTERTAINMENTS, AND FESTIVITIES

Djibouti Diabloins [*Little devils*]. Back: Carte Postale. (Undivided Back. Mailed 1906.)

15. Congo Français – Vive la France toujours! [*Long live France forever!*] – Brazzaville. Collection Leray. (Divided Back.)

71 La Prière [*Prayer*]. Collections ND Phot. Back: Carte Postale. Ce côté est exclusivement reserve à l'adresse [*This side is reserved exclusively for the address*]. Etablissements Photographique de Neurdein Freres – Paris. (Undivided Back. Mailed 1904.)

163. Sénégal – Dakar – [Procession].
Fortier, Phot., Dakar. (Undivided Back.)

Les Circoncis [*The newly circumcised*].
Maison Robert Schléber, Kayes. Back:
Carte Postale. Tous les pays n'acceptant
pas la correspondance au recto, se renseigner à la poste [*All countries do not accept
correspondence on the recto, inform yourself
at the post office*]. (Divided back.)

Afrique Occidentale – Soudan. 1118. Tam-Tam de Habbés (ces tam-tam sont allégoriques et présentent de nombreuses phases [Habbés drumming session (these sessions are allegoric and have numerous phases)]. Collection Genérale Fortier, Dakar. Back: Carte Postale. Tous les pays n'acceptant pas la correspondence au recto, se renseigner à la poste [*All countries do not accept correspondence on the recto, inform yourself at the post office*]. (Divided Back.)

457. Afrique Occidentale Française – Tam-Tam d'Enfants [*Children's drumming session*]. Collection Générale, A. O. F., Fortier, Dakar – Réprod. interd. Back: Carte Postale. (Divided Back)

151 Nègres au Café Maure [*Blacks in a Moorish café*]. "Oran 13 mai, 1904 and illegible signature." Collections ND Phot. Back: Carte Postale. Ce côté est exclusivement reservé à l'adresse [*This side is reserved exclusively for the address*]. Etablissements Photographique de Neurdein Frères. – Paris. (Undivided Back. Mailed 1904.)

138 A – Nègres au Café Maure [*Blacks in a Moorish café*]. Back: Carte Postale. Post Card Postkarte Briefkaart – Postkaart Cartolina Postale – Trajeta Postal. (Divided Back.)

Soudan [handwritten]. Back: Carte Postale.
Dernier repas d'adieu au Soudan [*Last farewell
meal in Soudan*]. (Divided Back.)

Zulus at Mealtime. "Mealie PAP."
550.700,.N. Back: Post Card. Printed
in Gt. Britain. The Valentine and Sons
Publishing Co. Ltd., P.O. Box 1685. Cape
Town. Copyright. (Divided Back.)

Missions Africaines, 150, Cours Gambetta, Lyon. Vicariat Apostolique de la Côte d'Ivoire. Une Fête à Adjamé. Notables buvant du Vin de Palme [*A feast in Adjamé with notables drinking palm wine*]. Back: Carte Postale. M. P. Bourgeois Frères, Chalons S.-S. (Divided Back.)

COPYRT. CAI. N. 71. Wedding Party, Civilized. Back: The SASCo. Real Photo Postcards. P.O. Box 5792, Johannesburg. For Inland Postage & some Foreign Countries the space below may be used for communication. (Divided Back.)

Carte Postale. Edição de Antonio Joao Simões – Moçambique PAP. Guedes – Lisboa. (Divided Back.)

1517. Afrique Occidentale – Dahomey – Abomey. – Danses des Féticheuses [*Dances of the Fetish worshippers*]. Collection générale Fortier, Dakar. Back: Carte Postale. (Divided Back. Mailed July 26, 2010.)

449. Afrique Occidentale Groupe de chefs Féticheurs [*West Africa. Group of Fetish-worshipping chiefs*]. Collection Générale Fortier, Dakar. Back: Carte Postale. (Divided Back.)

1503. Afrique Occidentale – Dahomey. Danseuses féticheurs, Région de Savallou [*Dance of the Fetish worshippers. Savallou Region*]. Collection générale Fortier, Dakar. Back: Carte Postale. (Divided Back.)

1516. Afrique Occidentale – Dahomey. Danses de féticheuses [*Dances of the Fetish worshippers*]. Collection générale Fortier, Dakar. Back: Carte Postale. (Divided Back. Mailed 26 June 1912[?].)

471. – Afrique Occidentale Française
Celles qui furent les Amazones
(femmes-guerriers redoutables
[*Those who were the Amazons, feared women warriors*]. Collection Générale Fortier, Dakar. Back: Carte Postale. (Divided Back.)

Ping Pong. Back: Post Card Address only to be written on this side. (Undivided Back. Mailed Durban July 26, 1903.)

The Kaffir's Piano. Back: Pictorial Card
(Undivided Back. Mailed May 30, 1903.)

II. SÉNÉGAMBIE-NIGER. – Joueurs de Balafons.
Cliché A. P., 25, rue de Trévise, Paris

II. Sénégambie-Niger. –Joueurs de Balafons
[*Balafon players*]. Cliché A. P., 25, rue de Trévise,
Paris. Back: Carte Postale, a utiliser seulement
dans la service intérieur (France, Algérie et Tu-
nisie) [*to be used only in interior service (France,
Algeria, Tunisia)*]. (Divided Back.)

48. Afrique Mystériense. – Les Coras.

48. Afrique Mystériense – Les Coras
[*The coras*]. (Divided Back.)

Griot. – St-Louis (Sénégal).

Griot. – St- Louis (Sénégal). Hostalier, St-Louis
(Sénégal). Back: Carte Postale. Ce côté est
exclusivement reserve à l'adresse [*This side is
reserved exclusively for the address*]. (Undivided
Back. Mailed 1904.)

The Caribbean

THE FARM, THE GARDEN, AND THE SEA

Tobacco and Sugar Cane Grove, Puerto Rico. Coleccion Paris – Bazar. Back: Puerto Rico Souvenir Card Trajeta Postal EHB559. (Undivided Back.)

Greetings from Jamaica. Pulping Cocoa.
"March 22, 1906. Had a pleasant afternoon.
Tomorrow take a long drive. Papa." No.5. A.
Duperly & Sons, Kingston-Ja. (Undivided
Back. Mailed 1906.)

Pulping Cocoa, Jamaica. "le 8 Mars 1906."
Back: Union Postale Universelle, Jamaica
(Jamaique) Post Card NO.14 J.W. Clary,
Kingston, Ja. (Divided Back. Mailed 1906.)

Breaking Cocoa Pods and crooking. "Always pleased to hear from you. This view shows Indian immigrants 'Men & Women' on a cocoa estate. Note – My name has no O in it. That's your only mistake." [Signature illegible]. Waterman, 15 Frederick Street, Trinidad. (Undivided Back. Mailed 1908.)

Drying Cocoa Beans, Trinidad, B.W.I. "All Rights reserved." Back: Muir, Marshall & co., Port of Spain, Trinidad. (Divided Back.)

Picking Pimento. Back: Jamaica (Jamaique)
Dr Jas. Johnson, Brown's Town, P. O. (Divided
Back. Made in Germany 4156.)

Martinique et Guadeloupe – Récolte de
manioc [*Manioc harvest*]. Édition Phos,
Pointe-à-Pitre (Guadeloupe). Reprod. interdite. Back: Carte Postale. (Undivided Back.)

Gathering Pineapples, Cuba. Back: Republica de Cuba Trajeta Postal Union
Postale Universelle (Post Card, Carte Postale) mailed from Santo Domingo
R.D. Oct 11, 19[??].

PLANTING SUGAR CANE IN PUERTO RICO.   1235

Planting Sugar Cane in Puerto Rico. 1235. Back: Post Card. Made in Germany. A. C. Bosselman & Co., New York. (Undivided Back.)

7002. Cutting Sugar Cane, Cuba.

7002. Cutting Sugar Cane, Cuba. Back: Republica de Cuba Trajeta Postal Union Postale Universelle (Post Card, Carte Post-ale). Published by Harris Bros. Co., Havana, Cuba. Made in U.S.A. 13808 Photochrome. (Divided Back.)

Cutting Sugar Cane, Barbados.

Cutting Sugar Cane, Barbados. Back: Post Card.
Published by Bruce Weatherhead, Barbados
Pharmacy. (Divided Back.)

MEANS OF TRANSPORTING SUGAR CANE, PUERTO RICO. 1233

Means of Transporting Sugar Cane, Puerto
Rico. 1233. Back: Post Card. Made in Ger-
many A. C. Bosselman & Co., New York.
(Undivided Back.)

Stacking Bags of Raw Sugar. Back: Post Card. British Manufacture. Printed for the Imperial Institute by McCorquodale & Co. Ltd. London. A Red Bromide Photograph. (Divided Back.)

The Caribbean

THE MARKETPLACE

"Greetings from Jamaica." Going to Market with Yams and Canes, Constant Spring Road. Back: Distributed by Jamaiça Views and Post Card Supplies, Kingston, Jamaica. Made in U.S.A. Obliterated Name. Post Card. Jamaica (Jamaique.) (Divided Back.)

Going to sell the Pig.

No. 89. Bannana Carrier, Port Antonio.

Going to sell the Pig. Back: H. G. Johnston, M. D. Brown's Town P.O. no 16. Union Postale Universelle, Jamaica (Jamaique). "Leaving today for the rest of the island. Don't expect much mail. Hope the heat in Phila. Is not too much for you. The pig in the picture might resemble my appetite. Mildred." [In different handwriting]: "I think there will be a famine in Jamaica because Mildred has eaten almost all the food. Everything is O. K. M.A.P. t-4138. (Divided Back. Mailed 1913.)

No. 89. Banana Carrier, Port Antonio. Back: Duperly & Sons Kingston, Jamaica. (Divided Back. Mailed 1909.)

"Greetings from Jamaica." Loading Banana, Port Antonio, Jamaica. Back: Union Postale Universelle. Post Card Jamaica (Jamaique). A. Duperly & Sons, Kingston, Ja. 4198. (Divided Back.)

Bermuda Fisherman, Bermuda. Rutherford. Back: Published by the Yankee Store & Bermuda Drug Co., Bermuda. No.72. (Divided Back.)

Coaling, St. Lucia. Back: This side may have a message written upon it for Postage the British Isles Only: The right hand side must be reserved for stamp and address. Transitional. (Divided Back.)

Banana Carriers, Jamaica. "XXXX Charlie 12.9.10." Back: Union Postale Universelle, Post Card Jamaica (Jamaique). Duperly, Kingston, Jamaica. (Mailed 1910.)

8272. Vegetable Men, Havana, Cuba.
Copyright, 1904, by Detroit Photographic
Co. (Undivided Back.)

Habana – A coffee plantation. J Charavay,
Obispo 131. [Illegible message in Spanish].
Back: Private Mailing Card. (Postal Card, Carte
Postale). This side is exclusively for the address.
(Undivided Back. Mailed September 26, 1902.)

CUBA – Chiva criandera III. – Nursing goat III. [Additional writing illegible.] Back: Trajeta Postal. Postal Card, Cuba.

The Caribbean

THE VENDORS AND THE COOKS

Market Women. David Arons, El Gusto Cigar Store, 6, King Street, Kingston, Jamaica. "After Aug. 11th my address will be P.O. Box 36 Barbados. This is just the way people take vegetables to market. Saturday is the day. MBS" Back: Union Postale Universelle, Jamaica (Jamaique) Post Card. (Undivided Back. Mailed 1903.)

Banana Seller. Greetings from Jamaica. Back: Post Card for Island postage. This space as well as the back may now be used for communication. (Divided Back. Mailed 1901.)

Martinique. 305 Collect. A. Benoit (Martinique). Une élégante Marchande de Bananes [*An elegant banana seller*]. Back: Carte Postale with message verso. (Divided Back.)

Street Vendor, Barbados, B.W.I.

E. 56 – Collect. A Benoit (Martinique). Martinique. Une de nos belles por-
teuses de charbon à la Cie Générale Transatlantique (à Fort-de-France.)
[One of our beautiful coal carriers at the General Transatlantic Company.]
"Ce sont les femmes qui font le gros travaux à la Martinique. Chaque
marne pleine pese 46k. Elles ont un sou par 2 marmes, elles en portent
une moyenne de 200 par jours ce qui leur fait environ 10000k portes
sur la tête." ["The women do the hard work in Martinique. Each full basket
weights 46 kilos. They get one sou per 2 baskets. They carry on average 200
a day which makes about 10000 kilos carried on their heads."] Back: Carte
Postale. (Divided Back. Mailed 1901.)

Street Vendor, Barbados, B.W.I. Back: Post Card ECO Canada. (Divided
Back.)

Bridgetown –Pottery Vendors. Back: A. E. Shannon 4 High Street, Bridgetown, Barbados Post Card. Made in France. (Divided Back.)

Pottery Vendors, Barbados. Back: Post Card 08 69660. (Divided Back.)

Martinique et Guadeloupe. Marchande de Simples [*Medicinal herb vendor*]. Edit. Phos, Pointe-à-Pitre (Guadeloupe). Back: Carte Postale. (Undivided Back. Mailed 1906.)

Guadeloupe – Marchande de Corossol [*Soursop vendor*]. Edit. Phos, Pointe-à-Pitre (Guadeloupe.) Back: Carte Postale. (Undivided Back.)

8. Guadeloupe – Marchande de Tablettes de Cocos [*Coconut candy vendor*]. Edit. Phos, Pointe-à-Pitre (Guadeloupe). Back: Carte Postale. La Correspondance au recto n'est pas acceptee par tous les Pays Etrangers Se rensigner à la Poste. [*Correspondence on the back may not be accepted by all foreign countries inform yourself at the Post Office*]. (Divided Back.)

Guadeloupe. – Marchande d'Acras [*Acras vendor*]. Edit. Phos, Pointe-à-Pitre (Guadeloupe). Back: Carte Postale. (Divided Back.)

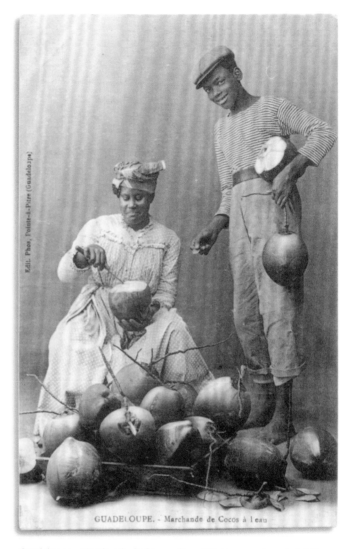

Guadeloupe – Marchande de Lait [*Milk vendor*]. Edit. Phos, Pointe-à-Pitre (Guadeloupe). Back: Carte Postale. (Divided Back.)

Guadeloupe – Marchande de Cocos a l'eau [*Water coconut vendor*]. Edit. Phos, Pointe-à-Pitre (Guadeloupe). Back: Carte Postale. (Divided Back.)

Négresses Marchandes Guadeloupe. [*Black women vendors*]. Back: Carte Postale. (Undivided Back.)

The Caribbean

LEISURE, ENTERTAINMENTS, AND FESTIVITIES

420. Guadeloupe – Chauds partisans de la canne à sucre [*Warm partisans of sugar cane*]. Editions Boisel, reproduction interdite. Back: Carte Postale. (Divided Back.)

A Dinner Party, Puerto Rico. Waldrop Photo Co., San Juan, P. R. Back: Post Card. (Divided Back.)

A Bunch of Coconut Pickers Puerto Rico. Back: Post Card. Made in Germany 3643. (Undivided Back.)

Negerhut – Curaçao [*Black person's hut*]. Penso & Delvalle, La Corona, Curaçao. "Curacao le 29.1.06. Placide." Back: Briefkaart uit de kolonie Curaçao. Carte Postale des Antilles neerlandaises. (Undivided Back. Mailed 1906.)

37. Approuague – La Danse du "Gragé." Phot. AB& Co. Nancy. "Mo prends oune charme / Pour mo charmé fille-là; / Mo réfléchi a rien de force pas bon; / Mo prends charme-là / Mo jeté-le dans la mer . . . / Si p'tite fille-là content mo, / Li ké marche derrière mo. (Air Créole)." Back: Carte Postale de la Guyana Francaise. (Undivided Back.)

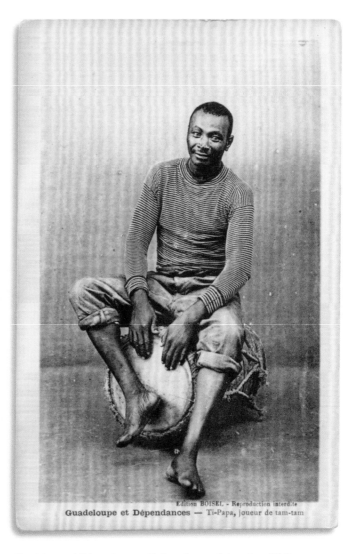

13815 Cigar Seller, Cuba. Back: Reupblica de Cuba (Trajeta Postal Union Postale Universelle. (Post Card, Carte Postale.) Published by Harris Bros. Co., Havana, Cuba. (Divided Back.)

Guadeloupe et Dépendances – Ti-Papa, joueur de tam-tam [*Ti-Papa – drummer*]. Edition BOISEL – Reproduction interdite. Back: Carte Postale Maison Ch. Boisel – Pointe à Pitre. Tout ce qui concerne la Photo.

18. Cayenne – Carnaval 1903. Mme Georges Evrard, phot. – Déposé. "Toute la nuit moin peux pas dormi, / A force doudou moin Ka chagriné moin, / Toute la nuit moin peux pas dormi, / A force doudou moin Ka chatouillé moin! / Ah! tanpis pour ça qui pas tini doudou, / Doudou moin dans bras moin! / Tanpis pour ça qui pas tini doudou, / Doudou moin, c'est tà moin!! (Air Créole.)" Back: Carte Postale de la Guyana Francaise. (Undivided Back.)

The Zapateo, Tipical [*sic*] Cuban Dance. Back: Union Postal Universal Post Card Republica de Cuba. (Divided Back.)

The Rumba. Back: Union Postal Universal Post Card Republica de Cuba. (Divided Back.)

Natives Representing Wild Indians on Carnival Day Trinidad, B. W. I. Back: Waterman, 15 Frederick Street, Trinidad, 1023 "Par Excellence." Printed in Germany. (Divided Back.)

E 37 Collect. A. Benoit Jeanette (Martinique.) Martinique – Une Ti Tane
[*A Ti tane*]. Back: Carte Postale. (Divided Back. Mailed 1931.)

Guadeloupe – Type no. 3. Edit. Phos, Pointe-à-Pitre (Guadeloupe).
Back: Carte Postale. (Undivided Back.)

Martinique. Type et Costume Créole [*Type and creole dress*]. Leboullanger, éditeur à Fort-de-France (Martinique) – 2017. Back: Carte Postale. (Undivided Back.)

Martinique. Un type de femme du pays [*A type of local woman*]. Leboullanger, éditeur à Fort-de-France. Back: Carte Postale. (Divided Back.)

57 Collect. A. Benoit Jeanette (Martinique.) Martinique –Femme en tête [Woman with head tie]. Back: Carte Postale. (Divided Back. Mailed 1930.)

E. 36. – Collect. A. Benoit (Martinique). MARTINIQUE. – Capresse en Costume du Pays [*A capresse en the dress of the country*]. Back: Carte Postale. (Divided Back.)

49 Guadeloupe – Type de Femme [*A type of woman*]. Back: Carte Postale. Levy et Neurdien reunis, 44, rue Letellier Paris. (Divided Back.)

Pointe-à-Pitre – Deux gentilles Guadeloupéennes. [*Two lovely Guadeloupeans*]. Edit. Phos, Pointe-à-Pitre (Guadeloupe). Back: Carte Postale. (Divided Back. Mailed 1908.)

Quatre types Guadeloupéennes [*Four types of Guadeloupeans*]. Nouvelle Edition de CATAN, photographe, Basse-Terre (Guadeloupe). Back: Carte Postal. (Divided Back.)

Martinique. Aux Antilles – Un Groupe d'Indiennes [*A group of Indian women*]. Back: Leboullanger, éditeur a Fort-de-France. Carte Postale. (Divided Back. Mailed 1911.)

8394. Polly in the Peanut Patch. Detroit Publishing Co. Back: Post Card.
(Undivided Back. Mailed 1905.)

Rice Plantation Scene. Back: 202810. Made in Germany. (Divided back.)

Bogging for Terrapin. Back: A. M. Barbee & Sons Terrapin Farm, Isle of Hope, Savannah, GA. (Mailed 1911.)

10274. Oyster Luggers at New Orleans, LA. Back: Post Card. (Undivided Back.)

Drawing the Seine at Ile of Palms, near Charleston, S. C. Back: Hugh C. Leighton Co. Manufacturers, Portland, ME, U.S.A. 23610. Made in Germany. (Divided Back.)

Strawberry Pickers, Florida. Back: Cochrane Co. Palatka, FLA. Made in U.S.A. copyright 1911 by Mann. (Divided Back.)

Strawberry Pickers and Crates, Norfolk, Va. 3054. "get to work negro's what do I pay you for, on a strike Emma." (Undivided Back. Mailed 1906.)

Among the Orange Groves in Florida. 117. Back: "The orange, a native of Asiatic Countries, was brought to America by the Spaniards in the 16th century. The blossoms are exquisitely fragrant with delicious white petals. A tree in all of its golden glory of ripened fruit is a delight to see." "Tichnor Quality Views" Tichnor Bros., Inc. Boston, Mass. (Divided Back.)

Washing Oranges, Florida. Back: Florida Artistic Series published by the H & W. B. Drew CO. Jacksonville, Fla. 1287. (Divided Back.)

A Beautiful Orange Grove in Florida.
Back: 1016 Florida Artistic Series. Florida Artistic Series. 1016. (Divided Back.)

Front: 13221. Potato Sorter and Sacker.
Back: Phostint Card Made only by Detroit Publishing CO. (Divided Back.)

Lettuce Field, Florida. Back: Florida Souvenir Post Card. 15266-Pub by Cochrane's Book Store, Palatka, Florida. (Divided Back.)

Sugar Cane Scene near New Orleans, La. Back: 17288 – Published by J. Scordill (2 Stores) 902 Canal ST., 701 Canal ST., New Orleans, LA. (Divided Back.)

Planting Sugar Cane. "Love from Grandma." Back: PLANTING SUGAR CANE. In the southern Section of the U.S. rattans or sugar canes must be planted every other year, the average growing season being about six months; the cane yields about 21 tons per acre. It was introduced into America in 1775, when eight slaves, skilled in its cultivation, were sent with it from Port au Prince, Hayti, to the Jesuit Fathers who planted it in what is now the first district of the city of New Orleans, LA. Post Card. Raphael Tuck & Sons' Post Card Series No. 2384 "Under Southern Skies." Art Publishers to Their Majesties the King and Queen. (Undivided Back. Mailed 1907.)

Cutting Sugar Cane. "Mrs Ed. Floyd. 12-18-07." Back: CUTTING SUGAR CANE. The sugar crop of the world aggregates about 10,000,000 tons or eight pounds per capita for the estimated population of 2,500,000,000. The U.S. consumes 70 pounds per capita one eleventh of which is domestic. The cane product is with difficulty holding its own against the beet sugar on account of the instability of labor. Post Card. Raphael Tuck & Sons' Post Card Series No. 2384 "Under Southern Skies." Art Publishers to Their Majesties the King and Queen. (Undivided Back. Mailed 1907.)

Preparing Turtle for Shipment, Key West, Fla. Back: Pub by S. H. Kress & Co. (Divided Back.)

Front: Unloading Watermelons, Pier "A," Newport News, Va. Back: Post Card Published by Louis Kaufman & Sons, Baltimore, MD. (Divided Back.)

UNLOADING WATERMELONS, PIER "A," NEWPORT NEWS, VA.

The United States

French Market, Vegetable Section. New Orleans, La. Back: Post Card. No. 2361. Adolph Setige Pub. Co. St. Louis. (Mailed 1907.) (Undivided Back.)

5362. FRENCH MARKET, NEW ORLEANS, LA.

5362. French Market, New Orleans, La. Copyright, 1900, by Detroit Photographic Co. (Undivided Back.)

French Market and Red Store, New Orleans, La.

French Market and Red Store, New Orleans, La. Back: Lipsher Specialty Co. 320 Magazine St., New Orleans, La. A-14961. (Divided Back.)

103 – French Market, New Orleans, La.
Back: Pub. by T.P. & CO, N.Y. (Divided Back.)

12313. Sixth Street Market, Richmond, Va.
Copyright 1908 by Detroit Publishing Co.
Back: "Phostint" card. (Divided Back. Mailed 1910.)

CHARLESTON, S. C. The Old Market.

Charleston, S. C. The Old Market. Printed in Holland. Back: "Section Old Market – This is the vegetable section where the old 'Maumas' presided over their stalls and dispensed their wares to merchants and professional men who, accompanied by their servants, were accustomed to make their own purchases in the old days." (Undivided Back. Mailed 1908.)

G 3676 Sugar on the Levee, New Orleans, La.

G 3676 Sugar on the Levee, New Orleans, La. Back: The Rotograph Co., NY, City. Germany. (Undivided Back.)

The United States

THE VENDORS AND THE COOKS

NEGRO VEGETABLE VENDOR, CHARLESTON, S.C.

Negro Vegetable Vendor, Charleston, S.C. Back: The Valentines & Sons, Printing Co., Ltd. New York. Printed in New York. (Divided Back. Mailed 1910.)

16801—Shrimp Vender

BASHFUL BILLY AND SISTER

5743. COPYRIGHT, 1902, BY DETROIT PHOTOGRAPHIC CO.

16801 – Shrimp Vender. Souvenir Post Card Co. N.Y. (Divided Back.)

Bashful Billy and Sister. 5743. Copyright, 1902, by Detroit Photographic Co. (Undivided Back.)

Shrimp Peddler, Charleston, South Carolina

Shrimp Peddler, Charleston, South Carolina. Back: Natural-Finis Card – Advertising Service Agency, Charleston, SC. (Divided Back.)

Milk Cart.   New Orleans, La.

Milk Cart. New Orleans, La. Back: 609216 published by The New Orleans News Company, New Orleans, La. Leipzig, Dresden. (Divided Back.)

Male Vegetable Vendor – An every morning scene on the Streets of Charleston, S.C. Back: The Hugh Leighton Co. Manufacturers, Portland, ME 26360. (Divided Back.)

Female Vegetable Vendors – An every morning scene on the Streets of Charleston, S.C. Back: The Hugh Leighton Co. Manufacturers, Portland, ME 26359. (Divided Back.)

10275. Milk Cart. New Orleans, La. (Undivided Back.)

Old Creole Praline Candy Woman, New Orleans, La. Back: CT American Art. (Divided Back.)

Vegetable Vender. Greetings from the Sunny South. 3163. Back: Made in Germany. A. C. Bosselman & Co. New York. (Undivided Back.)

16804 – Nut Cake Vender. Souvenir Post Card Co. N.Y. (Divided Back. Mailed 1909.)

Praline Vendor. New Orleans, La. Back: 14-7. F. M. Kirby 7 Co. (Divided Back.)

Praline Seller. New Orleans, La. "With love to you & your mother. J.S.R." Back: 6085/14. Published by the New Orleans News Company, New Orleans, LA. (Undivided Back. Mailed 1907.)

Old Time Kitchen & Darkey (Over 70)
Dixie Land. Back: 5665 Adolph Selige,
Pub. Co St. Louis – Leipzig. (Divided Back.
Mailed 1907.)

Old Southern Kitchen and Negro Mammy.
12525. (Divided Back. Mailed 1912).

Court Yard Kitchen. 820 St. Louis Street New Orleans, La. Back: Court Yard Kitchen. 820 St. Louis Street, New Orleans between Bourbon and Dauphine serves luncheon and afternoon tea by the open fireplace or out in the court-yard which is one of the beauty spots of the Vieux Carre. (Divided Back.)

The Nu-Wray Inn, Burnsville, North Carolina.

The Nu-Wray Inn, Burnsville, North Carolina. Back: The Smoke House at the Nu-Wray Inn. Will, (The colored chef), bringing hickory-smoked hams from the century-old smoke house. Hundreds of hams are cured each year by this old fashioned method and served daily in the Nu-Wray dining room. (Divided Back.)

ROASTING OYSTERS, CASINO, CAPE HENRY, VA.

Roasting Oysters, Casino, Cape Henry, Va. © H. C. Mann. Back: "The roasting of oysters forms an interesting subject for all visitors to this noted resort which adjoins the historic Light houses at Cape Henry." Published by Louis Kaufmann & Sons, Baltimore, MD. (Divided Back.)

Norfolk Natives. Norfolk, Va. Back: Published by Louis Kaufmann & Sons, Baltimore, MD. (Undivided Back. Mailed 1915.)

The United States

LEISURE, ENTERTAINMENTS, AND FESTIVITIES

No. 11. Roustabouts at Leisure. Back: Adolph Selige, Pub. Co. St. Louis – Leipzig. (Divided Back. Mailed 1909.)

Food for contention.

Food for contention. Back: L.114 W. G. MacFarlane, Publisher and Importer Buffalo and Toronto. (Undivided Back. Mailed 1907.)

Blackville Serenade in Florida.

Copyrighted 1892 by Havens.

Blackville Serenade in Florida. Copyrighted 1892 by Havens. Back: Florida Souvenir Post Card. 12811 – Pub by Cochran's Book Store, Palatka, Fla. (Divided Back.)

6470. A Happy Family. Copyright, 1902, by Detroit Photographic Co. (Undivided Back.)

Music Hath Charms. Back: A-1349. (Divided Back.)

The Coon Creek Rehearsal. Copyrighted by O. P. Havens 1893 Back:
(12813-1919.)

A Society Cake-walk of the "Upperten
duskies" of the New South. Newport
News, Va. Back: No. B14140. Published
by James E. Abbe, Newport News, VA.
(Divided Back.)

SOUTHERN DINNER TOTER MACON, GA.

M. BARNETT
OFFICE 40 ST LOUIS ST.

The Old Slave Block in the old St. Louis Hotel, New Orleans, La. The colored woman standing on the block was sold for $1,500.00 on this same block when a little girl. 264

WORKS CONSULTED

Bassett, Fred. "Wish You Were Here!: The Story of the Golden Age of Picture Postcards in the United States," http://www.nysl.nysed.gov/msscfa/qc16510ess.html.

"A Brief History of the Postcard." http://www.libanpostcard.com_history.html.

Geary, Christraud. "Different Visions: Postcards from Africa by European and African Photographers and Sponsors" in *Delivering Views: Distant Cultures in Early Postcards*, ed. Christraud Geary and Virginia Lee Webb. Washington: Smithsonian Institution Press, 1998.

Geary, Christraud. Postcards from Africa: Photographers of the Colonial Era. Selections from the Leonard A. Lauder Postcard Archive. Boston: MFA Publications, 2018.

Prochaska, David, and Jordana Mendelsson, eds. *Postcards: Ephemeral Histories of Modernity*. University Park, PA: Pennsylvania State University Press, 2010.

Smithsonian Institution Archives. "Dating Postcards," http://siarchives.si.edu/history/exhibits/postcard/dating-postcards.

Smithsonian Institution Archives. "Evolution of the Smithsonian Postcard," http://siarchives.si.edu/history/exhibits/postcard/postcard-history.

Thompson, T. Jack. "Communications from the Field: Missionary Postcards from Africa," in *Light on Darkness?: Missionary Photography of Africa in the Nineteenth and Early Twentieth Centuries*. Grand Rapids, MI: Wm. B. Eerdmans, 2012.

Titus, Felicitas. *Old Beijing: Postcards From the Imperial City*. North Clarendon, VT: Turtle, 2012.

Weaver, William Woys. *Culinary Ephemera: An Illustrated History*. Berkley, CA: University of California Press, 2010.

Willoughby, Martin. *A History of Postcards*. Secaucus, NJ: Wellfleet P, 1992.

Credit: Rog Walker of Paper Monday

ABOUT THE AUTHOR

Jessica B. Harris holds a PhD from NYU, is professor emerita of English at Queens College, and lectures internationally. The author of the memoir *My Soul Looks Back* as well as twelve cookbooks, her articles have appeared in *Vogue, Food & Wine, Essence*, and the *New Yorker*, among other publications. She has made numerous television and radio appearances and has been profiled in the *New York Times*. Considered one of the preeminent scholars of the food of the African diaspora, Harris has been inducted into the James Beard Who's Who in Food and Beverage in America and the James Beard Cookbook Hall of Fame, received an honorary doctorate from Johnson & Wales University, and recently helped the Smithsonian Museum of African American History and Culture conceptualize its cafeteria.